The One Thing:
Christ in You.
The Hope of Glory.

By Milt Rodriguez

Paperback – ISBN: 979-8-9905782-5-8
eBook – ISBN: 979-8-9905782-4-1

Layout and Cover Design: Michael Michelson

For retail or wholesale orders please contact: (Permissions also)
Jon Zens
C/O Searching Together
P.O. Box 548
St. Croix Falls, WI 54024
jzens@searchingtogether.org

Published in the United States by Ekklesia Press, Kearney, NE

First Printing: Nov. 2025

FOREWORD

I first met Milt and his wife in a living room in Gainesville, FL. I was visiting with the intention of moving there to be a part of group that was forming. The night we met I believe he was speaking on our "location" as believers. It was an extraordinary message on being "in Christ." That sparked a relationship that is still going on to this day. I am proud to say that Milt is my mentor, but more like a surrogate father. I would not be the man I am without Milt Rodriguez and his late wife Mary.

I have been a part of two churches where Milt has been one of the planters. The first was in Gainesville, FL, in 2009 where Milt was one of four planters. The second was in Nashville, TN, in 2011 where he and his wife were the planters. My experience of Jesus in these groups marked a drastic change in my life and helped shape who I am today.

In 2014, Milt sent out messages to all the churches he had been involved with (approximately ten or so at the time) saying that the Lord had moved him to begin training workers. The Lord called me to answer. I left everything that I knew with the Lord thus far, and moved to California to start training. There were six of us, two families and two single brothers.

We went to plant an amazing group of saints in Manteca, California. There, the trainees witnessed Milt plant a group from the ground up, start to finish. The one thing that I always remember about that first time was Milt telling us that he had no idea what he was doing—that the training would be from the power of the Lord and not from Milt himself. In Milt's mind, he was simply facilitating a place for the Lord Himself to train us through him. I very much believe he succeeded.

Almost a year later we went to Southern California to begin planting two churches simultaneously in Orange, California and Menifee, California. We lived, worked jobs, and planned for these groups together living in Corona, California. It was extraordinary.

I could go on. In a nutshell, the experience I had with Milt and Mary was like nothing I'd ever heard before, except from the New Testament stories themselves. The funny thing is, that is not what we were setting out to do. We were following our Lord with all our hearts, with everything that we had, holding nothing back.

And that describes who Milt is and what he continues to do.

The One Thing comes from the pen of a brother who has endured some of the most unimaginable, heartbreaking circumstances. He lost his wife during Covid without being able to be with her during her passing. His mother passed away two weeks later. In recent times he has had to face health challenges. These are merely a few of the insurmountable circumstances he faced. To be honest, Milt and Mary faced and overcame many terrible trials. They would tell you that they only made it through by the Lord's own life.

Despite all the things that happened to Milt, despite his incredible losses, I found him at the end of it all saying to me, "I am compelled to write and preach about Christ and His Church. What else can I do?"

I challenge you not to take for granted this honest and unfiltered work that a brother has put to ink when his entire world has crumbled around him. This book may seem simple. It may seem even a little light-hearted. But behind all the words are a man who has shined the light of Christ when all the darkness has come crashing down on him. I pray that Christ speaks to you and pulls you deeper into knowing Him more.

This book is not merely the message of Milt Rodriguez. Milt completely embodies this message. He lives it: Jesus Christ is The One Thing.

—Wes Saunders, Texarkana, Arkansas

The One Thing:
Christ in You.
The Hope of Glory.

By Milt Rodriguez

(Edited by Alison Hardy & Jon Zens)

Ekklesia
Press

Opening Thoughts

I want to share a message that's been on my heart for quite a while, which is kind of a hard message, but I'll try to be as winsome with you as I can. In my over twenty-five years working with groups meeting outside the traditional, institutional church system, I have seen many wonderful, glorious things, but I have also seen the problems that arise up close and personal. Most of the problems in these groups—in fact, most of the challenges in all of Christianity—come down to one main issue, and that's what I am addressing in this book—*the one thing: Jesus Christ.*

First, I want to go over some concepts that will be helpful in understanding the heart of this book.

The Word "Church"

Let's start by looking at the word "church." Where did this word come from and why do we use it so often?

When you see the word "church" in the New Testament, it is being translated from the Greek word *ekklesia*, which means a gathering in a particular place. *Ekklesia* is not a religious word. In Paul's opening of the letter to the Corinthians the typical translation says, "To the church of God which is in Corinth." A better translation would be, "To the gathering of God, which is in Corinth."

In the New Testament, *ekklesia* was never used to refer to a building. It is also not a place where people come to sit in pews, sing a few songs, listen to a sermon, throw a few bucks in the offering plate, and then go home. It also doesn't resemble an institution, a worship service, a one-person show, an entertainer with an audience, or a people wo hardly know one another. The way most of us think of and use the word "church" is totally foreign to what we read in our New Testaments. The first century church was nothing like that. Instead, Peter describes it as "a chosen race, a royal priesthood, a holy nation, a people for His own possession, that you may proclaim the excellencies of Him who called you out of darkness, into His marvelous light" (1 Pet. 2:9).

The word "church" is an unfortunate translation for *ekklesia* that has taken on new meanings over time. Because of Paul's writings we know of many other proper terms that can be used, such as body, bride, household, kingdom, saints, members (of the body), temple, and called out ones. Simply by using the apostle Paul's descriptions of the *ekklesia* we will begin to see, by God's Spirit and grace, the true definition, description, and revelation of God's eternal purpose in His body. I will use many of these words in this book, all referring to God's *ekklesia*, even using the word "church," but hopefully now you will know what I mean when I use the word.

The groups I have worked with over the years have met outside the institutional religious system, ideally without human agendas and traditions involved. A pure, natural expression of the church is what we're talking about here, without the human structure, organization, and institutionalism. It is an expression where Jesus Christ is the head, not just in theory, but in living experience. The *ekklesia* of God, as described in the first century writings, centered on Christ.

Jon Zens shows that there is much more connected to the word *ekklesia* than going to a building and working your way through an "order of service."

> Out of many choices, Jesus selected this word to define His building project. In light of all the revealed dimensions, *ekklesia* must be defined as *the Lord's people gathered together to carry out the whole gamut of Christ's kingdom purposes.* Matthew 18:15-20

shows that the saints comprise a problem-solving community. Notice that the *body* handles the issue. There is nothing in the passage about "the leaders" doing anything. The concern is brought to the *ekklesia*. Paul's letter to the Corinthians also shows that the *ekklesia* is called upon to deal with a wide spectrum of thorny issues (*Jesus Is Family: His Life Together, 2017, pp. 32-33*).

Maybe you are wondering why I work with groups outside the institutional religious system, proclaiming the eternal purpose of God and Christ Jesus as all. It's because I understand everything is about:

- This *ekklesia* of God, the one that functions out from the life of Christ within us.

- This *ekklesia* of God, the one that functions out from His headship and leadership.

- This *ekklesia* of God, without hierarchy, clergy, or laity in which all of the believer's function by the life of Christ in them and under His direct headship.

- This *ekklesia* of God, who is learning to abide in Christ, the vine, and live by His life.

- This *ekklesia* of God, who is not intimidated by polls, surveys, the public opinion, and what's popular or not popular.

- This *ekklesia* of God, who is the expression and direct reflection of her Lord Jesus the Christ.

- This *ekklesia* of God, who is the means to manifest the kingdom of God on earth.

- This *ekklesia* of God, who is the absolute fullness of the glory of her Christ.

Paul further explains: "To me, though I am the very least of all the saints, this grace was granted and graciously entrusted: to proclaim to the Gentiles the unending riches of Christ, also to enlighten all people and make plain to them what is the plan of the mystery kept hidden through the ages and concealed until now in God who created all things by Christ Jesus, that through the *ekklesia* the profound, many-sided wisdom of God in all its infinite variety and innumerable aspects might now be made known to the angelic rulers and authorities in the heavenly sphere. This is in accordance with the terms of the eternal and timeless purpose which He has realized and carried into effect in Christ Jesus our Lord, in whom, because of our faith in Him, we dare to have the boldness of free access" (Eph. 3:8-12).

This purpose, in a nutshell, is why I cannot and will not, as long as I have breath in my body, cease from proclaiming this "mystery" which Paul tells us is "Christ in you, the hope of glory" (Col. 1:28). This is the "church" that I will live for and die for as long as I am on this planet. I don't care what others are doing or saying. I don't care how much it cost me or how much time it takes. Just to make things clear, I am really only doing this for one simple reason: It is the will of God in Christ Jesus—His very heartbeat! How could I do anything else?

The Eternal Purpose Of God

When I say, "God's eternal purpose," most Christians haven't the foggiest idea what that is. You talk to a Christian about the eternal purpose, and they think, "It's about going to heaven. I'm going to have a mansion in the sky," like God is a Beverly Hills type of God. That is a terrible image, by the way.

God's eternal purpose is that the fullness of His Son, the Lord Jesus Christ, would be displayed and expressed visibly through a vessel that would be a family and house for the Father, a bride and body for the Son, and a temple for the Holy Spirit. The purpose was to create a race of redeemed humans that would both express both His nature and character, and represent His authority over the earth.

God's purpose could never be accomplished by human life on its own. It would take a much higher life than that. It would take God's very own life—divine life, eternal life, uncreated life. Human life is a lower life form that could never fulfill God's purpose or satisfy His heart. Preachers will stand up in front of people every Sunday morning telling them that they need to do more and to do better to be good Christians. The problem is that all of those people have the wrong life form to live that way. They are being asked to please God with their human life. Impossible.

Genesis 2 tells us the way God is going to accomplish this purpose. He offered the first couple to ingest His very own life. He placed them before the tree of life (Jesus Christ). The obvious implication here is that they would eat of that tree and thereby take the life of God into their being, so that they would be able to live by that life and thus accomplish God's eternal purpose.

The Community of God
God is not a "loner." He is a community of three Persons who are one: the Father, the Son, and the Holy Spirit. This is not something that we can learn by any kind of human understanding. It must be given by the grace God through His Spirit. That can only take place by the humble heart seeking earnestly after God's eternal purpose.

This is the absolute key to understanding the lifestyle of God! He is not a solo act. He is not a hermit in the woods. He is not a loner-type God who would prefer to live alone in a tiny cabin. He is a corporate God who loves to love others. And He created us to be like Him, to be in a community, to love and be loved.

The core and center of this God is family, togetherness, oneness, corporateness, giving, and sharing His life. In fact, sharing all that He is with His creation is His very nature. Just stating that He is a "good God" is not even in the ballpark of spiritual reality. He's more than great. He's more than wonderful. He's more, more, more than anything or anyone you could imagine. He is *the all* of creation, both visible and invisible. He is *the all* of time and eternity. In fact, all of these things are inside of Him.

Lord Jesus, I ask that those who read this book will be touched by your Spirit to see and hear these things like it was their first time. Lord, may they not think, "Oh yeah, I know that," but instead humbly, like a child, receive what you have said as if they had never heard or read it before. And Lord, may it cause a complete revolution to take place in their hearts and within your body throughout the world. Amen.

The One Thing

There are many issues surrounding being the church, the *ekklesia* of God, but I'm going to focus in on one particular issue. I believe this is the issue that is the biggest hindrance to authentic church life, especially in America. This is the major obstacle to Christ actually getting the expression from His church that He's desiring.

To help explain both this hindrance and the solution, I'm going to refer to a movie that came out in 1991 called *City Slickers*. I like movies and this is a funny one. The plot of the movie is centered around three guy friends and who go on some kind of adventure together once a year.

When the movie starts, the main character, Mitch, is having a midlife crisis. He loves his family, but he's got a really dead-end job and he's lost purpose and motivation in his life. He's going on this trip in hopes that something happens.

They go on a two-week cattle drive from New Mexico to Colorado, and, of course, all kinds of adventures and challenges happen. But there is a particular scene that stands out to me.

The guy who is in charge of the cattle drive is an old cowboy named Curly. He's a tough guy, and one of the last real cowboys. In this scene, Mitch is spending time with Curly. Mitch is telling him his dilemma, that he's got a dead-end job, and that he doesn't have any purpose in life now. The exchange between the two goes like this (edited for content):

Curly: Do you know what the secret of life is? [He holds up one finger] This.
Mitch: Your finger?
Curly: One thing. Just one thing.
Mitch: But what is the one thing?
Curly: [smiles] That's what you have to find out.

The rest of the movie is about Mitch discovering what the one thing is.

I want to talk about the one thing. There really is only one thing. Thank God it's that simple; the Lord has given us the simplicity of Christ.

The One Thing is a Person

I'm going to start in Psalm 27:4, "One thing I have asked from the Lord, that I shall seek after: that I may dwell in the house of the Lord all the days of my life, to behold the beauty of the Lord...."

That's where you find the beauty of the Lord, by the way, it's in His house. You've got to be in His house to see how beautiful He is. Why? Because He is expressed through all the saints. The "house of the Lord" is not a building or a temple. It is the place where living stones gather together.

So here's the one thing according to David: That I may dwell in the house of the Lord all the days of my life, to behold the beauty of the Lord.

It was said of Jesus, that "zeal for Your house consumes Me" (Psalm 69:8; John 2:12). Such commitment to the house of God was more than evident in David. In Psalm 132:3-5, he exclaimed, "I will not go home; I will not let myself rest, I will not let my eyes sleep nor close my eyelids in slumber until I find a place to build a house for the Lord, a sanctuary for the Mighty One of Israel."

Later in life, he uttered these words, "In addition, in my delight in the house of my God, the treasure I have of gold and silver, I give to the house of my God, over and above all that I have already provided for the holy temple." And then his words to the prophet Nathan: "Here I am living in a palace of cedar while the Lord has no resting place" (2 Samuel 7:2).

May the zeal for the Lord's House that marked Jesus and David be expressed by the Spirit in our lives as we throw aside every hindrance that would threaten our commitment to be in line with Jesus' purpose to build His house, the *ekklesia*.

Now let's travel to the New Testament, where Paul is writing to a group of believers in Phillippi. "For me to live is Christ and to die is gain..." (Phil. 1:21). And later John quotes Jesus, "Whoever has seen me has seen the Father" (John 14:9).

In these writings, Paul and Jesus Himself make it very clear that *Jesus Christ* is the one thing. Not just teachings about Jesus Christ. Not theology or messages about Jesus Christ. Jesus Christ, the Person. He, Himself, is the one thing. And the reason the early church was so blessed in spiritual power was because they believed this, and they practiced it. They made Him their *one thing*.

The person of Jesus Christ is the one thing:
- He is the reality of the authentic and true Canaan Land (Col.1:12)

- He is the reality and fulfillment of Light (Col. 1:12)

- He is the real beloved referred to in Song of Solomon and He is the true King (Col. 1:13)

- He is true redemption and forgiveness (Col.1:14)

- He is the reality of the full expression of the Father (Col. 1:15a)

- He is the firstborn, the model, the pattern for all of creation (Col. 1:15b)

- For all creation is by Him, for Him, and through Him (Col. 1:16).

- He is before all things (Col. 1:17a)

- He is the glue that holds all things together (Col. 1:17b)

- He is the head of the body, the church (Col. 1:18a)

- He is the beginning, the firstborn from the dead (Col. 1:18b)

- He will come to have the first place in all things (Col. 1:18c)

- All of the fullness was pleased to tabernacle (dwell) in Him (Col. 1:19)

God's purpose in creation was so that this one Person would be expressed. His purpose in redemption was that this one Person would have a counterpart and that she (the bride) would fully express Him. His purpose in sanctification and transformation was that this one Person would increase and come to fill all things with Himself. God's purpose in healing was to express that one Person who himself is health. His purpose in salvation was to enlarge and expand that one Person who is salvation.

Jesus Christ is the all of God and the all of God's purpose and plan. There is no other person that God is interested in or concerned about. Yes, He loves the whole world but only in and through this one person!

This is very important to realize. You can't study this. You can't know Him with your head. You can't know Him with your emotions. You can't know Him with your will. You can only know Him with one vehicle, and that is your spirit. You see, you have a spirit inside of you that God gave you, a human spirit. And God has a spirit, right? When you come to Christ, the two become one. He turns water into wine. How does He do it? He introduces a new element to the water. We're just water. But He brings Himself, the new wine, and adds His life to us, to our spirit. And now we're one spirit.

Jesus Christ is God's one thing. It makes sense that He would be our one thing, too, doesn't it?

One spirit. The one thing.

One Mind, One Heart, One Purpose
Next, let's go to Philippians 2, starting verse 2, "Make my joy complete by being of the same mind, maintaining the same love, united in spirit, intent on one purpose. Do nothing from selfishness

or empty conceit. But with humility of mind, regard one another as more important than yourselves. Do not merely look out for your own personal interests, but also for the interests of others." Being of the same mind. Maintaining the same love. United in spirit. Intent on one purpose. Do you see sameness here? Do you see oneness here? What does it speak of to you? First of all, it speaks to me of singleness, singularity. Singleness of heart. Singleness of focus. Singleness of purpose. Singular vision.

I got saved and grew up in a really remarkable time in Southern California in the 1960s and 1970s, referred to as the Jesus People Movement. Eventually it went worldwide, and I believe it was a true movement of God. Yes, there was a lot of craziness that happened because hippies were getting saved and lots of young people were coming to Christ. But there was this singleness of purpose among those people, and that really impressed me, because they were excited about the Lord. They were on fire. They were radicals for God. They were revolutionaries for Jesus. And God did a lot of things during that time.

In Acts 2:46-47 Luke describes an early gathering of Christ=followers, saying, "Day by day, continuing with one mind in the temple, and breaking bread from house to house, they were taking their meals together with gladness and sincerity of heart, praising God and having favor with all the people. And the Lord was adding to their number day by day those who were being saved." Many translations, instead of using the word "sincerity," say "singleness" of heart.

Singleness. One heart. One purpose. Also, single-mindedness. James says a double-minded person is unstable in all his ways. Guess what, saints? We are double-minded people. Let's be honest about this. We need to have one focus. One purpose. One mind. The mind of Jesus Christ. This is easier said than done, of course. Only God can do this. The church is unstable because the church has a double mind.

We talk about the difference between the institutional church and groups that meet outside the religious system. And guess what? The same problem exists in both. Double-mindedness. Or maybe triple- or quadruple-mindedness. God has made it so simple. The church of Jesus Christ, the *ekklesia* of God, is a single-minded people. People with a single focus. The one thing.

One spirit. One mind. One purpose. One heart. The one thing.

One Goal

Still in Philippians, now in chapter 3, starting at verse 7, it says, "But whatever things were gain to me, those things I have counted as loss for the sake of Christ." Speaking of radicals and revolutionaries, this guy Paul was one.

"More than that, I count all things as loss in view of the surpassing value of knowing Christ Jesus my Lord." And that knowing is a deep word. It's a knowing experientially, not just knowing in the head. The head doesn't really help here. It's a spiritual thing.

"For whom I have suffered the loss of all things and count them but rubbish." Some translations use the word dung.

"So that I may gain Christ, and may be found in him, not having a righteousness of my own derived from the law, but that which is through the faithfulness of Christ. The righteousness which comes from God on the basis of faith. That I may know him and the power of his resurrection, and the fellowship of his sufferings, being conformed to his death. In order that I may attain to the resurrection from the dead. Not that I have already obtained it or have already become perfect. But I press on, so that I may lay hold of that for which I was laid hold of by Jesus Christ." I love that phrase: That I may lay hold of that for which I was laid hold of by Jesus Christ.

Why did he lay hold of you? Why did he grab you? There's a reason. He did it for one purpose—for the one thing. It's very simple really.

"Forgetting what lies behind and straining forward to what lies ahead, I press on toward the goal for the prize of the upward call of God in Christ Jesus. Let us therefore as many as are perfect have this attitude. And if in anything you have a different attitude, God will reveal that also to you. However, let us keep living by the same standard to which we have attained" (Phil. 3:13-14).

One spirit. One mind. One purpose. One heart. One goal. The one thing.

One Vision, One Focus

Singular vision is important. In the Song of Songs, it talks about having dove's eyes. A dove has peculiar eyes; a dove can only focus on one thing at a time. And doves, by the way, mate for life. They have one mate for the rest of their lives. Whenever you see a dove, you'll always see another dove. They're always together. And they have singular vision. That's why in the Song of Songs it talks so much about the dove and the dove's eyes. Singleness of vision, singleness of focus.

One focus means no distractions. When you're focused on one thing, it's easy to focus on it. If I'm looking at one person, then I can't look anywhere else. If I look anywhere else, I'm distracted, right? And the way our minds work, they can only focus on one thing at a time anyway. Do you realize this? You can try little exercises to test this. Start by counting in your mind. It doesn't take much effort, it's almost automatic, right? Then, while you are still counting, have someone ask you a question. See if you can answer their question and still keep counting. You can't do it. Our minds are made to focus on one thing at a time. God made us that way for a reason, didn't He?

One spirit. One mind. One purpose. One heart. One goal. One vision. One focus. The one thing.

One Body

Oneness and togetherness are very important in the Lord's house. All of the parts of the body must depend upon each other in order that Christ would have His suitable expression. These parts flow together in the spirit by something called "agape love." That is, by laying down their lives for one another. This "one anothering" is one of the pillars of body life. Being the body of Christ is a way of life.

Functioning as the body of Christ is not attending a meeting once per week. It is not going to a building once a week and listening to a sermon, singing a few songs, and then going home until next week. Can you imagine the following scene? Once or twice a week your physical body disassembles, and all the parts of your body go to different buildings in different parts of town. Can you imagine what that would be like? That's not a real body at all. That's just body parts scattered all over town trying to be spiritual.

True spirituality is based upon the Spirit of God, and He would never separate and be so dysfunctional. It's way past time for us to get a powerful revelation and vision of God's eternal purpose: That He would be expressed through a body of people who are all living and functioning as His body under His direct headship.

"For as the body is one and has many members, but all the members of that one body, being many, are one body, whether Jews or Greeks, whether slaves or free—and have all been made to drink into one Spirit. For, in fact, the body is not one member but many" (1 Cor. 12:12-14). From here, Paul goes into describing the other parts of the body and how they all need one another and should care for one another. Then he goes into describing the different giftings and how they all complement one another and need one another.

Speaking very clearly and boldly here: How can anyone read Paul's description in 1 Corinthians 12 and claim that he is describing a bunch of people sitting in pews in a building with one person up front doing all the functioning? Paul is describing something totally different. He is describing a body made up of humans who have the living Christ inside of them. Each of them is both spiritually and practically the body of the living Christ. Is this glorious or what? Is this awesome or what? Is this really rare on the earth or what?

One spirit. One mind. One purpose. One heart. One goal. One vision. One focus. One body. The one thing.

One House

The true *ekklesia* of God that we read about in our New Testament is nothing like what we now see around us in the present religious system. It's none of the following: a physical building, an organization or business, a "service" or meeting of some kind, a hierarchical system whereby there is some kind of chain-of-command, where you submit to someone and they submit to someone else, hence, an authoritarian system. Let me be clear: There is no such thing as a "church building." There is no such thing as a "sacred building." The *ekklesia* is not anything conceived or constructed by humankind. Unfortunately, the true *ekklesia* of God that we read about in our New Testament is nothing like what we now see around us in the present religious system.

As I mentioned before, the word *ekklesia* in the Greek means an assembly or gathering. Of course, in the first century they had many kinds of gatherings for many different purposes. There were assemblies for family gatherings, governmental meetings, political meetings, educational gatherings, business meetings, and on it goes. There were also gatherings of the people of God.

These gatherings, the *ekklesia* of God, were built and are being built together into one house for the Lord. "So then you are no longer strangers and aliens but you are fellow citizens with the saints [God's holy people] and are members of God's household, having been built on the foundation of the apostles and prophets, with Christ Jesus Himself as the Chief Cornerstone, in whom the whole structure is joined together, and it continues to increase growing into a holy temple in the Lord. In Him and in fellowship with one another, you also are being built together into a dwelling place of God in the Spirit" (Eph. 2:19-22).

The *ekklesia* of God is built together into one house for God. When Jesus and the apostles spoke and wrote about *ekklesia*, they were referring to a spiritual, Godly, and heavenly type of meeting. Even though these gatherings were happening on earth, there was much more happening in the heavenly realms. That is the kingdom of heaven happening on this earth.

One spirit. One mind. One purpose. One heart. One goal. One vision. One focus. One body. One house. The one thing.

What is Your One Thing?

Let me ask you this. What is your *one thing*?

It's easy to say "Jesus." But what is the one thing that occupies your time? The one thing that occupies your thoughts? The one thing that occupies your energies? See, this becomes very practical, doesn't it?

When we work with groups, the one problem we run into the most is saints not having enough time, saints being too busy. They say, "Oh,

I can make it to a meeting once a week." And that's why the Sunday morning service works so well. Why not? Who does anything on Sunday morning? You read the newspaper, maybe have breakfast, or watch a football game. A Sunday morning service works really well in our culture. It fits in with the lifestyle. But suggest getting together any other time, "Well, I just don't know how. I'm really busy." What are you so busy doing? And how important are all those things you're doing? How important are they in God's heart, in God's mind?

What is your *one thing*?

The First Thing

The one thing is not only the one thing. It's also the first thing. The first thing reveals a little bit of a nuance, doesn't it? What does "first" remind you of? How about priority? It's first. It comes before anything. That's what "first" means.

Jesus said, "Seek first the kingdom of God and His righteousness and all these things will be added to you" (Matt. 6:33). Seek *first*. Seek first what? Seek first His kingdom and His righteousness. Righteousness speaks of the character of God, who He is. It's interesting to me that He puts His kingdom first, even before Himself. He says, "Seek first the kingdom of God and His righteousness." Why is that? Because the kingdom is the most important thing to God. It's His kingdom, His bride, His body, His house, His community, His city. So, what's a kingdom? It's a civilization. It's a society, right? It's a society of people who have one ruler, the king. Seek that first. Why? Because that's what God's seeking first. That's His eternal purpose. That's why He put you here. That's why you're breathing air right now. That's why you wake up every morning. It's not for you. It's not for this world system. It's for the kingdom. And guess what? Jesus is the kingdom.

Remember when He was standing there amongst the Pharisees? He said, "the kingdom of God is among you." Some translations say, "the kingdom of God is within you." That's incorrect. He wouldn't say that to the Pharisees, believe me. But He did say, "The kingdom of God is among you [in your midst]." How could He say that? Because He was standing in the middle of them. They really didn't get it.

So why is the Kingdom of God first? Because Jesus Christ is the kingdom. So that's why we can say, "Seek first the kingdom," because it's Him. He has this whole society inside of Himself.
But He wants it expressed, right? He wants it expressed on the earth in a very practical, physical way, as well as spiritually.

Permit Me First
In Luke 9:59, we have Jesus speaking again. "[Jesus] said to another, follow me. But he said, 'Lord, permit me first to go and bury my father.'"

See the *first* there? That's why it's not only about the one thing, but about the first thing. We put other things first, don't we? That's an issue. That's a problem. We have to have singular focus, singular purpose, singular mindedness.

Was this a bad guy? No. He wanted to go bury his dad. What's wrong with that? His dad just died. The problem was he said "first." Jesus said, "follow me." He said, "I'd really like to but, *first*, I have to go do this one thing."

There were a lot of people that came to the Lord who said, "I have to do this first." It wasn't just this one guy. And he told them all the same thing: Let the dead bury the dead. We might think, "Lord, that's kind of harsh." No, it isn't. He's the Lord of lords, He's the King of all kings, isn't He? He's the creator of this universe. Is anything He asks of us too much? No. And it works because He gives us Himself—He gives us the strength to carry it out. It's all Him. All He wants is our willingness to put Him first as the one thing.

This is a matter of a heart condition, isn't it? That's what we're talking about here. We're not saying you can't bury your dad. That's not what the Lord is talking about. He's talking about you having singleness of heart, having Him as first place in your life.

First in Value

"The kingdom of heaven is like a treasure hidden in a field, which a man found and hid again and from joy over it goes and sells all that he has and buys that field. Again, the kingdom of heaven is like a merchant seeking fine pearls, and upon finding one pearl of great value, he went and sold all he had and bought it" (Matt. 13:44-46).

What are these verses speaking of? Value, right? These guys found something of value: treasures, pearls. And what did they do? Sold everything they had to purchase them. This speaks of firsts. This speaks of priority.

What are the things you value the most? Jesus touched upon every area of life, didn't He? He dealt with relationships, with family, with culture and possessions. He hit on every area of life that we value. He said, "That thing is okay. But you're not going to seek that first. I come first. I'm the pearl of great price. I'm the treasure buried in the field. Go and sell everything you have to purchase that field." It's not just any treasure—it's *the* treasure, saints. It's an eternal treasure; it's not going to wear out.

First speaks of importance. First speaks of quality. First speaks of priority. First speaks of capturing your attention. First in your thoughts, first in your time, first in your energy. Seek first the kingdom of God.

Seeking Other Things First

One of the main issues blocking the true expression of Jesus Christ on this earth, especially in America, is that we are so busy seeking other things. We are so busy putting our life energies, our money—everything—into other things except the one true thing that matters. How could we be so foolish? It doesn't even make any sense, does it?

Henri Nouwen put his finger on a huge issue regarding our busyness.

> From a distance, it appears that we try to keep each other filled with words and actions, without tolerance for a moment of silence . . . . being busy, active and on the move has nearly become part of our constitution. When we are asked to sit in a chair, without a paper to read, a radio to listen to, a television to watch, without a visitor or a phone, we are inclined to become so restless and tense that we welcome anything that will distract us again. This explains why silence is such a difficult task . . . . Our preoccupations help us maintain the personal world we have created over the years and block the way to revolutionary change (*Reaching Out*, 1975, pp. 52-53).

Most Western believers are preoccupied with their thing instead of the one thing. In the Gospels Jesus calls us very clearly to drop everything to follow Him. Why would we follow Him? Because He's going somewhere. Where is He going? He's going to build a city, a house, a body, a bride. He clearly stated His singular purpose: *I will build my ekklesia*. That's where He's going. That's what He's doing. Drop everything to follow this guy. He is your one and only true Lord. He is your life.

Again, the phrase I hear more than anything when we're planting a church is, "I'm too busy." Anybody can go to the meeting once a week—just about anybody, even top executives can fit that into their schedule. But that's not what the Lord's after. He's after a people who are completely His in every way.

"Drop everything."
"No, I just can't do that."

Yes, you can. God never asks you to do something you can't do. He gives you the ability to do it. He gives you the grace and strength and the power to do it because it's Him working inside of you. But *you* have to actually be willing to let go of all the other things. And when we're talking about the *ekklesia* of God, a group meeting outside of the religious system, this is especially true, because we're not talking about a meeting once a week—we're talking about a life together, we're talking about community.

You can't have community once a week with people. You can't have community when everybody lives forty-five minutes away from each other. "What? You're saying we should move?" If necessary. Yes, drop everything. "Milt, that's crazy, that's radical." I know. I'm not the first guy to say this, I'm just a repeater. I'm just repeating what the Lord said: Drop everything to follow me.

The Headship of Jesus Christ
"And He put all things under His feet, and gave Him to be head over all things to the church, which is His body, the fullness of Him who fills all in all" (Eph. 1:22-23).

"And he is the head of the body, the assembly. He is the beginning, the firstborn from the dead, that in everything he might be preeminent" (Col 1:18).

It is totally fitting that Paul would tell the Ephesians and Colossians that Christ is the head of His Church, which is His body. Did you get that, dear saint? The *ekklesia* of Jesus Christ is not a building or a service on Sunday with pews and a pulpit. The *ekklesia* is not an organization, a business, or a corporation. The *ekklesia* of Christ is not a denominational hierarchy or some kind of club. God forbid! In fact, God is ashamed of our ideas and concepts of the "church." We have made a mess of things because our very carnal minds take the thoughts and concepts from the world system and try to apply them to God's holy body and bride.

"For in Him all the fullness of Deity dwells in bodily form, and in Him you have been made complete, and He is the head over all rule and authority" (Col 2:9-10).

The *ekklesia* of God is a gathering of people that keep Jesus as the functional head of His church If Jesus is really the first thing, He makes all the decisions. That's what a head does. He's in charge, right? We take that very seriously, that he's in charge. Practically, then, how do we make decisions under the headship of Christ? All the saints seek the Lord. They all seek the mind of Christ together and find out what He wants on any given subject or decision.

We see the church seeking the mind of Christ together in Jerusalem concerning the decision to not place any additional burdens on the new believers who were Gentiles. "Then it seemed good to the apostles and the elders, with the whole church, to choose men from among them to send to Antioch with Paul and Barnabas— Judas called Barsabbas, and Silas, leading men among the brethren" (Acts 15:22). In this passage, those who have itinerant ministries, mature saints, the whole church, and the Holy Spirit are all agreeing together on the mind of Christ. That's how decisions were made under the headship of Jesus Christ.

So, it still is today, Jesus does not express His headship through human-based, top-to-bottom, chain-of-command style leadership. There is no one human person who leads or directs His church—that would be putting that human first.

We hold in very high esteem the practice of the whole body seeking the Head for His direction and decisions. This can be a very long and arduous task. It's actually very simple to explain, but not simple to do. The brothers and sisters in the church get together for a specific purpose of making decisions and planning. If the church is healthy, then the members of the body will have already been seeking the mind of Christ about the matters to be discussed ahead of time and will come to the gathering with a sense in their spirits of what the Lord is saying. They will already have spent time in fellowship and prayer with the Lord about the matters to be discussed. This can be a difficult process, and sometimes it takes a while, but the group does not move ahead until the body agrees on what the Lord wants.

Believe it or not, you will make fewer mistakes that way because it's not one person making the decision, or even a council of people. Some things have to be hashed out, and of course you have the human element involved in all that, so it's not necessarily an easy process. Yet, it's all of the saints coming together after seeking the Head, finding out what His mind is, and making the decision.

His mind can be discovered in the midst of believers who have humbled themselves to the Lord and submitted themselves to one another under his direct Lordship and headship. His headship can be real and functional for those who put Him first and seek out his indwelling, eternal, uncreated, divine life together so that He can fully be expressed on the earth again.

The Body of Christ

Jesus said, "I and the Father are one." Why could He say this? Because He's in the Father and the Father's in Him, so being in one another makes us one.

Jesus Christ is one with His body. Is this true? I hope so. The head is one with the body. We don't really want a headless body—that's scary Sleepy Hollow type stuff, you know? So, Jesus Christ is one with His body. Of course, we don't really think that way, do we? "Well, there's the church here and then Jesus the head is up in heaven." Well, yes, He is in the heavens, but He's a pretty powerful God. He can be in more than one place at a time, and He is also in us on the earth, with those who are born into His kingdom.

This body of Christ is the *ekklesia*. This body is made up of many parts or members. Each and every part is filled with Christ by means of the Holy Spirit. Christ is the head and we, the believers, are His "members."

When you want to move any part of your body, what is the first step? Doesn't it have to begin in your mind? If you want to move your right arm, then the first step is for your head to think the thought first. Is this not true? The head has to think the thought first and then your arm responds.

Following our line of thought about Christ (the head) and the church (the body), we can say that if communication is lost between the head and the body then we have a real problem!

Not only must there be good communication between head and body, but there must be the true and solid laying down of our lives for one another. Or in a one-word summation: love. This is why the apostle Paul tells us in 1 Corinthians 13 all about God's eternal love. Right after Paul explains in chapter 12 about how the body functions, he tells us in chapter 13 all about God's agape love.

You could say that the energy that moves and empowers the *ekklesia* is this agape love. It is the very love of God Himself. It is the love that is the spiritual "glue" that holds the Godhead together. It is the "glue" that holds the community of God together. And it is a community.

We cannot display to the world this incredible "body life" if we are all living our own independent, separated, isolated, individual lives. Putting Christ first means putting His body first—head and body cannot be separated: "...so that there would be no division or discord in the body [that is, lack of adaptation of the parts to each other], but that the parts may have the same concern and love for one another" (1 Cor. 12:25, Amp.).

Paul's comparison of the human body to the body of Christ in 1 Corinthians is both ingenious and inspired by the Holy Spirit. This is all about the life of Christ within us. And it is His Spirit within us that brings this life. But this life needs to have an expression. It needs to be seen in the world around it. God wants to be expressed, and His body is the way it happens, just like your physical body expresses the person who lives inside. God, in Christ, wants to have His expression as well. That happens through His body, the *ekklesia* of God.

How does this visible expression of the living Christ come about? All true believers have Christ living in them. But in order to have the body we must *live* Christ. That is, each member of the body must be living by the Spirit and life of Christ. All true believers have Christ, but are we *living* Christ? All the members of the body must be active and grow. If there is no growth, then the life of the body will become stagnant, and the body will be paralyzed.

Living Temples
"Don't you know that your body is the temple of the Holy Spirit, who lives in you and who was given to you by God? You do not

31

belong to yourselves but to God; He bought you for a price. So, use your bodies for God's glory" (1 Cor. 6:19-20).

By the way, what is the hope of glory? Christ in you is God's hope of being seen—that is, expressed in our realm. So, what does it mean to be a temple of the Holy Spirit? Being a temple of the Holy Spirit is you being the house of God, the human carrier of the whole Kingdom of God! It is you making Christ the first thing, in the way He designed it, by expressing His life.

This *is not* you going to a building on Sunday morning sitting in a pew staring at the back of the head of the person in front of you, listening to that sermon, and passing the plate. I don't know about you, but I really get no life whatsoever by that kind of ritual. God never intended or designed it that way.

He placed His precious Son inside of us, the temple of the Holy Spirit. And when that happened, we became vehicles of the Spirit. Just think, you have the living God inside of you. You can participate in so much life and edification of the Spirit just by sitting in a living room with five other saints, with all of you functioning as members of His body by sharing His life with one another, face to face.

"Surely you know that you are God's temple and that God's Spirit lives in you. So, if anyone destroys God's temple, God will destroy him. For God's temple is holy, and you yourselves are His temple" (1 Cor. 3:16, 17).

There are no buildings on this planet that are holy. It's man-made religion that believes that. That's why Paul tells us in 1 Corinthians 3 that only God's temple is holy, and that the temple is the people that are in Christ and have Christ in them. I don't care how beautifully "holy" a building has been made to look with the stained-glass windows, beautiful drapes made of satin and velour, solid oak altar and pews, and candles lit all around—it's all still wood, hay and stubble!

Being a temple of the Holy Spirit is a people making Jesus Christ the first thing. First speaks of importance. First speaks of quality. First speaks of priority. First speaks of capturing your attention. First in your thoughts, first in your time, first in your energy. Seek first the kingdom of God.

God's concern is our hearts, that is the center of our being or our spirit, where God's Spirit dwells. Dear brothers and sisters, just think of it: the God of all creation has chosen to live (dwell) in us. Wow, who would have thought? Obviously, He did!

The Only Thing
The one thing is not just the one thing or the first thing; it's also the *only* thing. This is a tough one (as if the others weren't).

"For to me to live is Christ and to die is gain" (Phil. 1:21). What a statement: For me to live is Christ. If I'm alive, it's Christ. My only life is Christ. My only hope is Christ. My only dream is Christ. My only vision is Christ. I don't have any other visions. I don't have any other purposes. I don't have any other goals in life—just one goal, Jesus Christ. Wow. That's quite a statement there, Paul.

You might be saying, "This guy sounds like a radical to me." Yeah, I'll say. He upset a lot of people, especially the Roman Empire and the Jewish religious system. That's why they were always after him. He paid a high price for this, making Christ the *one thing*, making Him the *only thing*. For me to live is *Christ, Christ, and only Christ*.

I'm telling you what it takes to be a functional *ekklesia*. I'm not going to water it down, folks. I'm not going to make it easier than the Lord has made it. In fact, it is impossible to do this.

People ask me, "Milt, is this difficult?" No, it's impossible. It's humanly impossible to do this. That's why it's so interesting— because the human element isn't involved. Only God can do it. God in you. Christ in you, the hope of glory.

Let's look at Colossians 3, verse 1. This is a very important factor in realizing the only thing, because if you don't get this, you will try to do it yourself.

"Therefore, if you have been raised up with Christ keep seeking the things above where Christ is seated at the right hand of God. Set your mind [it also can be "affections"] on the things above, not on the things that are on the earth. For you have died and your life is hidden with Christ in God" (Col. 3:1).

What, you have died? Yes. Do you realize you're dead? I mean really realize it, by revelation? It's one thing to say, "Theologically, I know Paul said we're dead." But when this really becomes a living reality in your life, you will realize you're a dead person in a deeper way.

When I plant a church, I always spend some time having the saints refer to one another as dead people and reminding one another that we are dead. The old man is dead, thank God. You don't need him dragging behind you.

"You have died, and your life is hidden with Christ in God." Isn't it beautiful? Your only life is hidden with Christ in God. "When Christ, who is our life..." See? Christ is your only life now. You have no other life. You hear people say all the time, "I have no life." Well, that's true of the believer. It really is true. I have no other life. Christ is my only life now. He's the only thing, the one thing. "When Christ, who is your life, is revealed, then you will also be revealed with Him in glory."

Galatians 2:20 drives the point home even more—it has a famous "first." You probably have it memorized. "I have been crucified with Christ. It is no longer I who live, but Christ lives in me."

There are two "I's" here in this passage. The first "I" is the old man, as in, "I have been crucified with Christ…" Then there is the second "I," starting at "Christ lives in me, and the life which I now live in the flesh, I live by the faithfulness of the Son of God, who loved me and gave himself up for me."

You see that switch there? There are two "I's" here. There's the old humanity. This person doesn't live anymore. He's dead. In the new humanity, the new creation, I am in Christ and He's in me, that's the new person. That's my only life now, the new creation, the new humanity. I have no other life.

For people who want to live in an authentic *ekklesia*, it's better their life's dead, buried, gone. So, when we say things like, "Well, you're going to have to give all your time to this," and we hear, "What? I can't do that." Why not? You're dead. Now your only life is Christ. He doesn't have time for His own church? I don't believe that. This gets real practical, doesn't it?

Jesus said, "Deny yourself and follow me." I don't know why or how this started, but this phrase, "I'm going to die to self, I'm going to learn to die to self," is a terrible phrase. The Scriptures never say, "die to yourself." That sounds like you are somehow going to be able to die to you. Good luck with that one.

The word there is "deny," and it literally means to disown. Disown yourself, because you no longer own yourself anyway. You belong to Him. Ownership has been taken away from you—the only life is Christ now. You no longer own your own life. Just to realize that, to live by that, is the key.

"Lord, I totally belong to you now. I no longer belong to myself." If you understand this, when He asks you to do something, it's no big deal because you're dead anyway. "Go do this, go do that," "I want you to say that to that person," "I want you to go to this country," whatever it is, you go and do. It's that simple. You don't own your life—He does. That's what the word "Lord" means—that He's in charge, right?

He Is Our Life
He is our life. He's in us and we're in him. But it's one thing to know that theologically and positionally, it's another to live it out practically. And living by His life is something nobody has the market cornered on. It's a process. It's a growth thing. And you will live your whole life and never get to the end of that. It's an eternal thing. His life, of course, is eternal. But what is the quality of His life? What are the factors of His life? What are the indications of His life? It's about learning all of those types of things and then living by that life instead of your own.

Living by the life of Christ is really important to be the church, to be the *ekklesia* of God, by the way. That a group of people coming together is the expression of Jesus Christ—and not the expression of me, or of you, or of a group of people—is essential.

The Center of the Church
Jesus Christ is not just our individual life now, but also the life and center of the church. That's not just a phrase that we throw around. We take that very seriously, that He is actually the center of our attention. He's the centerpiece on the table. We're all looking at Him all the time and learning how to behold Him. That word "behold" means to intensely gaze upon Him and participate with Him in the gazing, and so it's seeing, but much more in-depth seeing than just

looking at something. He is the center of our lives individually and together as the church.

It's not enough just to have close relationships and a tightly-knit group. The one factor binding us together must be Christ Himself. We should not be together because we all get along and have the same interests. That would be a social group, not the *ekklesia* of Jesus Christ.

What transforms us is the internal life of Christ within us all. This is a together thing. His image is corporate, so doesn't it make sense that the process of conforming us to that image would also be corporate?

The Bride of Christ

"Isn't she lovely? Isn't she wonderful? Isn't she precious?"
-*Isn't She Lovely?* by Stevie Wonder

Even though the great lyrics to this song penned by Stevie Wonder are very beautiful, they do not even come close to any words attempting to describe the beauty of the Lord's own bride, His glorious Church, the Ekklesia.

Now, some of you reading this book might be offended with the thought that Jesus Christ has a wife, but guess what? It's the absolute truth. In fact, this is an eternal truth that's been in the heart and mind of the Father since before creation. God came up with the idea of oneness for humans. He was already three-in-one, so it only makes sense that His bride would also be made of many who are one.

She is a beautiful maiden. But we don't see her in the traditional, institutional, hierarchical system that we call "church." Driving to a building once per week, sitting in a pew, listening to a sermon, and then going home is not functioning as the bride of Christ. This is in no way God's thought about His bride. Simply put, this rendition of "church" is more like a pathetic, weak, bony, cross-eyed wrinkled old hag.

Where is the beautiful maiden? Where is the true Sarah when we need her? Where is the woman at the well? Where is the faith of Rebekah when we need her? Where are the Ruths who are willing to change their minds completely about who God is and enter into God's kingdom on earth? Where are the sisters who are in Christ and members of Christ's body and bride? And where are the brothers, the husbands, who will encourage and backup their precious sisters and wives for Christ and His bride?

Counting the Cost

"Now large crowds were going along with Him. He turned and said to them, 'If anyone comes to me and does not hate his own father and mother and wife and children and brothers and sisters, yes, and even his own life, he cannot be my disciple'" (Luke 14:25-26).

Did Jesus really say this? It's in the Bible, folks. I have proof. Mine isn't a red-letter, it's just black letters, but it's in there. This is radical stuff, is it not?

"Lord, you can't really mean that. It's just figurative language, right?" He meant it. We are supposed to have singular focus, and that singularity isn't physical family. Yes, I really said that. Our focus is not our family.

Our focus is *the* family—His family. And it begins with Him, doesn't it? Because He is the family. And the fact is that we are already connected, we are already united with Him. We are in Christ and He is in us. This makes us one (John 17:22-23). How could we all be "in Christ" and not be one? The problem is not our oneness, the problem is the practical expression of that oneness. That comes through us walking it out together day by day. That comes through us developing a "body consciousness" as Watchman Nee called it. It comes through a revelation of the corporate nature of the *ekklesia* of God. It comes through developing a lifestyle of community, and not one of individualism and independence. And it comes by us sharing our lives with one another and taking care of one another. In a word, this is family, but family in the true sense of the word. Not family as we have seen it in this world, but family as a genuine expression of the community life of God.

"If anyone comes to me and does not hate his own father, mother, wife, children, and brothers and sisters..." and, don't forget, "*even his own life*, he cannot be my disciple." He is saying that you can't even follow Him if you don't leave everything. He will not allow anyone to follow Him that doesn't lose everything. But remember, Jesus promised that those who lose physical family for His sake will receive a hundredfold of brothers, sisters, moms and dads *in this life*.

Where did we ever get the idea that we could follow Christ without denying ourselves? From insipid, lukewarm Christianity, that's where. This gospel in mainstream Christianity preached to us that isn't about the lordship and the kingship of Jesus Christ at all. We're still king, we're still lord, we just include Him now in our lives. "Oh, isn't He wonderful? Jesus, I love Him. He's healing me, He's helping me." It's about us.

Now let's add the next verses in Luke, "Whoever does not carry his own cross and come after me cannot be my disciple." This requires a death to your own life, to the world system, to everything but Him and His purpose. You must count the cost to follow Him. "For which one of you when he wants to build a tower does not first sit down and calculate the cost to see if he has enough to complete it?" Makes sense, doesn't it? Don't you do this with everything? You're going to build something, you're going to create something, you've got to figure out the cost. "They ridiculed him saying, 'this man has begun to build and was not able to finish,' or what king, when he sets out to meet another king in battle, will not first sit down and consider whether he is strong enough with ten thousand men to encounter the one coming against him with twenty thousand." Not too bright, is it? You have to count the cost or else "while the other is still far away, he will send a delegation and asked for terms of peace."

That just fits an American lifestyle completely, doesn't it? I can hear the reply now, "This is too radical. Lord, I just I don't know if we can handle this." How might Jesus respond? "Therefore, salt is good, but even salt, if even salt has become tasteless with what will it be seasoned? It is useless either for the soil or for the manure pile. It is thrown out. He who has ears to hear let him hear" (Luke 14:34-35).

You're worthless to God if you're distracted by other things because there is only one thing, saints, and that one thing is also the first thing, and that first thing is also the only thing—*Jesus Christ*.

"Yeah, wow, you're crazy, Milt. You really are crazy." Yes, I am. We used to say, "I want to be crazy. I want to be bonkers for Jesus." That was in the Jesus People days. It was considered to be a good thing because only a crazy person would do what Paul did. Only crazy people would do the things those early Christians did and live the way they lived. And everybody around them said, "Well, they're definitely peculiar, aren't they?" That was a nice way of saying, "These guys are nuts." They didn't get it; they didn't understand it. But that's okay because there has always been a testimony on the earth, a true, genuine expression of the Lord's Kingdom, the Lord's house, on the earth, although it has always been small. Very small.

In Christianity, we need people who are sold out to Christ. We need people who are radical for the kingdom. We need people who are revolutionaries. It's not about you going out and doing your ministry. I'm not saying ministry won't be done, but it's not about that. It's about Him getting His church, His house, His bride, His city, His society, His kingdom, His expression, His New Jerusalem. It's about the church, the *ekklesia* of God. She is the city set on a hill; she is the light of the world. That's what He wants. That's what's going to affect the world—not some personal ministry or missionary endeavor. Read the New Testament, brothers and sisters. It's always corporate. It is "we," not "me."

If we would just be the City of God, people would go, "Wow, who are these people? Look at the way they love one another. Who does this? Everyone else is into themselves, into their own thing." The one thing is "their own thing" for many people. Is it for you? Is your one thing you and your life?

Your Life
A key to living by this new life is setting your mind on things above not on things on the earth. It's setting your mind, your heart, your life on Jesus Christ. Becoming a Jesus person.

"That person is into Jesus. All they care about is Jesus."
"Wow. That person's a weirdo."

Yes, we look weird to the world, don't we?

There is something that's going to hinder God getting His purpose, His kingdom, His house, His bride, His body, but it's not the enemy and it's not the religious system. The only thing that can hinder God from getting His eternal purpose on the earth is *your life*. Now understand me here: All of God's plans are going to be accomplished, for He declares "the end from the beginning" (Isa. 46:10), but His way and means for getting His desires on earth involve His *ekklesia* functioning by His life. And what gets in the way of a believer functioning by the Lord's life? Their life. That's why He told you to lose your life. Unless you're willing to lose your life, you will not gain the kingdom. That's pretty direct, isn't it? Lose ownership of yourself because you don't really own yourself anymore anyway.

Your life is the thing getting in the way, and we see this all the time. We start a group. It's all exciting in the beginning. Everybody's, "Yeah, Jesus! Jesus, He's the Lord! He's the center! He's the head! He's the life!" And then nobody shows up for a meeting. It's like, "What happened? Where is everybody?" Well, they were out doing things.

And it's not about a meeting, it's about a life. But meetings are part of that life, getting together is part of that life. You can't have the church without getting together. If you're going to have a family, family gets together, right? Family gathers and eats together. That's very important. In fact, if you read the Book of Acts, you see they were getting together all the time, daily. And that got people's attention. There were thousands of people and they were sharing homes and meals. There was this new society, this new community, a city within the city. This was happening in Jerusalem, the center of Old Testament Israel.

They were radicals and they turned that city upside down, didn't they? Everywhere they went, it was said of Paul and his associates, "Oh, there are those guys that turn those cities upside down." They were known to be the turner-upside-downers. Why were they? How could they do that?

They were sold out to Jesus Christ. He was the one thing, the first thing, and the only thing in their lives. In fact, they no longer had a life—He was their life now. This singular Jesus-life was noted by Karen Mains:

> All their service, all their time, all their belongings, all their talents were interpreted in light of the definitive manifesto: You are not your own. You were bought with a price. You are bondslaves of Christ Jesus! . . . All we have belongs to Him—our clothes, our time, our families, our cars, books, inheritances, and homes (*Open Heart—Open Home*, David C. Cook, 1976, pp. 55, 58).

I want to see people like that again. We saw it briefly in the Jesus People movement. We've seen it a little bit in some of what we've been involved with. I want to see it take over the earth. I believe that's the Lord's heart—that the New Jerusalem comes down to earth. Don't be looking forward to going to heaven—heaven's coming to earth. May your kingdom come, your will be done, on earth as it is in heaven.

Is Christ Enough?

This is a clarion call. I'm calling you to turn from your life, to turn from your busy, busy world, to the Kingdom of God, to His eternal purpose, to what God wants, and become passionate for that instead of your thing—forget your thing.

God will take care of your thing, believe me. Seek first the kingdom, and guess what? All those other things you seek after all the time, He'll take care of those. I have tested that year after year after year and God comes through every time. If we will seek first His kingdom, He will take care of all of our stuff that we're so concerned about all the time.

Don't take one thought for all of that other stuff, and especially do not worry about it. Is it going to add anything to our lives? No. It's just worry. Why do we worry? Because we really don't believe He can

43

do it. We really don't trust Him to do it. He's not enough. We don't even really believe what Jesus and the New Testament writers said. That's because if we did, then our lives would be very different than a typical Christian of today. We would be radical, even revolutionary people. Instead, what we see around us today is this insipid, anemic, lukewarm version of so-called Christianity, and, for the most part, a people who are not willing to lose anything, let alone their very lives.

I can honestly say that I believe the main problem with believers who are attempting to return to a genuine, authentic, New Testament expression of the church is that they are just not willing to lose their lives. They can often say the right words, but they are often not willing to actually deny themselves and put Christ as the one thing, the first thing, the only thing. They do not trust that Christ is enough to take care of everything and fulfill all His promises.

Remember, if you're really busy seeking first the kingdom you won't even have any time to think if He's going to take care of your other things or not. There will be no time to worry about those things. He will be the focus and the rest will be taken care of.

One of the first things that happens when I come to plant a new church is I tell the believers that they will need to clear their schedules and simplify their lives. I also tell them that the church cannot be just an adjunct or add-on to their lives. The church must now be their lives. I can honestly say that most people don't experience true *ekklesia* simply because they are willing to live without it. You must be desperate for this life. I mean really desperate.

Remember:
- We are all called to follow Him completely by giving up our lives and living by His life

- We are all called to forsake all to follow Him

44

- We are all called to take up His interests and His purpose and lay down all of our ideas, dreams, hopes, agendas, programs, wants, and even needs

- We are all called to take up His all-encompassing interest, which is His church

- We are all called to go wherever and do whatever He needs for His eternal purpose (the expression of Christ in His body)

In other words: A true follower of Christ is someone who has given up all rights to himself and his or her own desires, wishes, dreams, and goals. Someone who has Jesus Christ as the one thing, the first thing, and the only thing. That's just being a normal Christian—but, unfortunately, "normal" is now viewed as radical.

I'm going to wrap up with another movie reference. One of my favorite movies is *The Untouchables* with Kevin Costner and Sean Connery. It's about law enforcement officers taking down one of the most notorious criminals of all time: Al Capone of Chicago. Costner (Elliot Ness) works for the Treasury department and has been commissioned to put Capone out of business. Connery (Jim Malone) is an older Irish cop on the beat in Chicago. He has obviously been around the block several times and knows what is really going on with crime in the city. Ness recruits Malone to help him take Capone down.

Malone wants to see how serious Ness is about facing Capone by asking him one simple question, "What are you prepared to do?" Malone then goes on to tell Ness that this is an all or nothing endeavor—that if he goes after Capone, it will cost him everything.

Brothers and sisters, what are you prepared to do? Are you willing to go wherever and do whatever your Lord wants? Don't answer too quickly! It's so easy to say "yes" to such a proposition without having counted the cost. And what is the cost? The cost is simply everything—your whole life. But it's worth it, because He's worth it.

We know for sure one person who got it right: Mary of Bethany. Jesus came into Martha and Mary's home, and Mary plopped herself down at Jesus' feet and heard His word. Martha complained that Mary was not helping, and Jesus replied, in a firm yet tender way as only He could, "Martha, you are concerned about many things, but there is *only one thing worth being concerned about.* Mary has discovered it, and it will not be taken away from her" (Luke 10:41-42). Mary indeed found the *one thing* that Curly told Mitch he had to find in *City Slickers.*

Is Christ really enough? Yes.

Lord, I want you to be the one thing, I want you to be the first thing, I want you to be the only thing in my life. I know now that I don't have my own life anymore. Consume me so it's no longer about me and my agenda and my plan for my life. I want everything to be about your kingdom, your purpose, your plan. May zeal for Your House consumes me!

One spirit. One mind. One purpose. One heart. One goal. One vision. One focus. One body. One house. The one thing. The first thing. The only thing. *Jesus Christ.*

For Further Reflection

Robert Banks, *Paul's Idea of Community: The Early House Churches in Their Cultural Setting*, 1979.

Del Birkey, *The Fall of Patriarchy: It's Broken Legacy Judged by Jesus and the Apostolic House Church Communities*, 2005.

Emil Brunner, *The Misunderstanding of the Church*, 1952.

Thomas Dubay, *Caring: A Biblical Theology of Community*, 1993.

S.D. Gaede, *Belonging: Our Need for Community in Church & Family*, 1985.

Carolyn Osiek, *A Woman's Place: House Churches in Earliest Christianity*, 2006.

Milt Rodriguez, *Eyes Wide Open: Seeing the Unseen*, 2023.

Milt Rodriguez, *The Community Life of God*, 2009.

Mark Strom, *Reframing Paul: Conversations in Grace & Community*, 2000.

Frank Viola, *Finding Organic Church*, 2009.

Jon Zens, *Jesus Is Family: His Life Together*, 2017.

Jon Zens, YouTube, "The Tucson Videos, #7, Jesus Is Building, But Not a Building," 2016.